THE UK
TOWER VORTX
DUAL BASKET
AIR FRYER COOKBOOK
WITH COLOUR PICTURES

Simple, Affordable and Delicious Air Fry, Bake, Roast and Grill Recipes for Anyone to Cook with Tower Dual Basket Air Fryer

Diane Jackson

Table of Contents

INTRODUCTION

Hello there, I'm Diane Jackson, and I want to share with you a story of how the Tower Vortx Duo Basket Air Fryer transformed my life and my family's happiness. My wife and I had just start-ed our family, and as much as we cherished the little one, our busy work schedules left us drained and exhausted by the time we got home. Cooking dinner felt like an insurmountable task, and it took away the precious time we wanted to spend together as a family.

Then, one day, the Tower Vortx Duo Basket Air Fryer entered our lives, and everything changed for the better. This incredible appliance made cooking a breeze, even for two tired souls like us. With its user-friendly design and the ability to prepare two delicious meals si-multaneously, it quickly became our kitchen savior. It allowed us to enjoy tasty, home-cooked meals without the exhausting preparation and cleanup that traditional cooking often entails.

As we embraced this newfound culinary convenience, we began experimenting with various recipes and discovered the joy of creating delicious, wholesome meals effortlessly. Over time, we compiled a treasure trove of simple yet delectable recipes, spanning from classic English breakfasts to mouthwatering desserts, snacks, and nutritious meat dishes. These recipes not only saved us time but also brought a sense of satisfaction and fulfillment back into our lives.

Now, I want to pay it forward. I want to share the recipes that have made our lives easier, more enjoyable, and our family happier. That's why I've put together this cookbook, filled with recipes designed for busy families like ours. Each recipe is carefully crafted with UK measurements and ingredients in mind, and I've included vibrant colour pictures to inspire your culinary adventures.

My hope is that this cookbook will find its way into the homes of more families, just like ours, who long for delicious, stress-free meals that bring everyone together. Let this cookbook be your guide to a more relaxed and enjoyable family life. Say goodbye to the exhaustion and hello to the joy of cooking with the Tower Vortx Duo Basket Air Fryer.

So, why wait? Dive in, explore these mouthwatering recipes, and experience the transformation for yourself. Embrace the convenience, savor the flavours, and relish the moments with your loved ones. Together, we can make family dinners a delightful and cherished tradition once more. Thank you for joining me on this culinary journey, and I can't wait for you to taste the happiness these recipes bring to your home.

CHAPTER 1
Breakfast

Ham and Corn Muffins

MAKES 8 MUFFINS

| PREP TIME: 10 minutes
| COOK TIME: 8 minutes

30 ml vegetable oil
180 g yellow cornmeal
120 ml milk
120 g shredded mature Cheddar cheese
120 g diced ham
30 g flour
6 g baking powder
¼ tsp. salt
1 egg, beaten

1. In a medium bowl, stir together the cornmeal, flour, baking powder and salt.
2. Add the egg, vegetable oil, and milk to dry ingredients and mix well.
3. Stir in shredded cheese and diced ham.
4. Divide batter among 8 parchment-paper-lined muffin cups.
5. When ready to cook, remove the grill plates and preheat the airfryer baskets for three minutes by activating the automatic preheat key.
6. Place 4 filled muffin cups in each basket. Select the Match Cook key then set basket 1 to 190°C for 8 minutes, then touch the start key to activate the airfryer. Bake until a toothpick inserted in centre of the muffin comes out clean.
7. When cooking is complete, transfer the muffins to a plate and serve warm.

Sausage Pitta Pizza

SERVES 4

| PREP TIME: 10 minutes
| COOK TIME: 6 minutes

15 ml olive oil
1 pitta bread
80 g sausage
225 g Mozzarella cheese
30 ml ketchup
1 tsp. garlic powder

1. Spread the ketchup over the pitta bread.
2. Top with the sausage and cheese. Brush with the garlic powder and olive oil.
3. When ready to cook, remove the grill plate from basket 1 then preheat the airfryer basket for three minutes by activating the automatic preheat key.
4. Place the pizza into basket 1 and set the temperature to 170°C for 6 minutes, then touch the start key to activate the airfryer.
5. When cooking is complete, transfer the pizza to a plate and serve warm.

Simple Coffee Doughnuts

SERVES 6

| PREP TIME: 5 minutes
| COOK TIME: 8 minutes

cooking spray
15 ml sunflower oil
120 g flour
60 ml coffee
50 g sugar
½ tsp. salt
5 g baking powder
1 tbsp. aquafaba

1. In a large bowl, combine the sugar, flour, salt and baking powder.
2. Add the coffee, aquafaba and sunflower oil and mix until a dough is formed. Leave the dough to rest in the refrigerator.
3. Remove the dough from the fridge and divide up, kneading each section into a doughnut.
4. When ready to cook, remove the grill plates and preheat the airfryer baskets for three minutes by activating the automatic preheat key.
5. Place half of the doughnuts in a single layer in each basket and spray with cooking spray. Select the Match Cook key then set basket 1 to 200°C for 8 minutes, then touch the start key to activate the airfryer. Carefully turn the doughnuts halfway through cooking using a silicone spatula.
6. When cooking is complete, transfer the doughnuts to a plate. Serve warm.

Delish Mushroom Frittata

SERVES 2

| PREP TIME: 15 minutes
| COOK TIME: 17 minutes

Cooking spray, as required
300 g button mushrooms, sliced thinly
3 eggs
½ red onion, sliced thinly
45 g feta cheese, crumbled
15 ml olive oil
Salt, to taste

1. Grease two 10 cm ramekins with cooking spray.
2. Heat the olive oil in a frying pan on medium heat and add the onion and mushrooms.
3. Sauté for about 5 minutes and dish out the mushroom mixture in a medium bowl.
4. Whisk together eggs and salt in a small bowl and transfer into the prepared ramekins.
5. Place the mushroom mixture over the eggs and top with feta cheese.
6. When ready to cook, remove the grill plates and preheat the airfryer baskets for three minutes by activating the automatic preheat key.
7. Place one ramekin in each basket. Select the Match Cook key then set basket 1 to 160°C for 12 minutes, then touch the start key to activate the airfryer.
8. When cooking is complete, transfer the ramekins and serve warm.

Cinnamon Toasts

SERVES 4

| PREP TIME: 5 minutes
| COOK TIME: 6 minutes

10 bread slices
15 g salted butter
60 g sugar
4 g ground cinnamon
½ tsp. vanilla extract

1. In a small bowl, combine the cinnamon, butter, sugar, and vanilla extract. Spread onto the slices of bread.
2. When ready to cook, remove the grill plates and preheat the airfryer baskets for three minutes by activating the automatic preheat key.
3. lace 5 bread slices in each basket. Select the Match Cook key then set basket 1 to 190°C for 6 minutes, then touch the start key to activate the airfryer, until golden brown. Halfway through cooking, flip the breads over.
4. When cooking is complete, serve warm.

Healthy Blueberry Muffins

MAKES 8 MUFFINS

| PREP TIME: 10 minutes
| COOK TIME: 15 minutes

80 ml rapeseed oil
100 g blueberries, fresh or frozen and thawed
160 g flour
120 ml milk
100 g sugar
1 egg
10 g baking powder
¼ tsp. salt

1. In a medium bowl, stir together flour, sugar, baking powder and salt.
2. In a separate bowl, combine the rapeseed oil, egg and milk and mix well.
3. Add the egg mixture to the dry ingredients and stir just until moistened.
4. Gently stir in the blueberries.
5. Spoon the batter evenly into parchment-paper-lined muffin cups.
6. When ready to cook, remove the grill plates and preheat the airfryer baskets for three minutes by activating the automatic preheat key.
7. Place 4 muffin cups in each basket. Select the Match Cook key then set basket 1 to 160°C for 15 minutes, then touch the start key to activate the airfryer, until tops spring back when touched lightly.
8. When cooking is complete, transfer the muffin cups and serve warm.

Cream Bread

SERVES 8

| **PREP TIME:** 20 minutes
| **COOK TIME:** 50 minutes

240 ml milk
1 large egg
415 g bread flour
180 ml whipping cream
70 g plain flour
50 g fine sugar
20 g milk powder
10 g dry yeast
1 tsp. salt

1. Grease two 18 x 10 cm cake pans.
2. Mix together all the dry ingredients with the wet ingredients to form a dough.
3. Divide the dough into 4 equal-sized balls and roll each ball into a rectangle.
4. Roll each rectangle like a Swiss roll tightly and place 2 rolls into each prepared cake pan. Keep aside for about 1 hour.
5. When ready to cook, remove the grill plates and preheat the airfryer baskets for three minutes by activating the automatic preheat key.
6. Place one cake pan in each basket. Select the Match Cook key then set basket 1 to 190°C for 50 minutes, then touch the start key to activate the airfryer. Bake until a toothpick inserted in centre comes out clean.
7. When cooking is complete, remove the bread rolls from pans. Cut each roll into desired size slices and serve warm.

Breakfast Bacon Frittata

SERVES 2

| **PREP TIME:** 15 minutes
| **COOK TIME:** 14 minutes

15 ml olive oil
50 g Parmesan cheese, grated and divided
1 rasher of bacon, chopped
6 cherry tomatoes, halved
6 fresh mushrooms, sliced
3 eggs
Salt and black pepper, to taste

1. Grease a 18 x 13 cm baking dish with olive oil.
2. Mix together tomatoes, bacon, mushrooms, salt and black pepper in the greased baking dish.
3. When ready to cook, remove the grill plate from basket 1 then preheat the airfryer basket for three minutes by activating the automatic preheat key.
4. Place the baking dish into basket 1 and set the temperature to 200°C for 14 minutes, then touch the start key to activate the airfryer.
5. Meanwhile, whisk together eggs and cheese in a bowl.
6. After 6 minutes, pour the egg mixture evenly over bacon mixture and cook for a further 8 minutes, until the egg is set.
7. When cooking is complete, serve warm.

Creamy Tomato Casserole

SERVES 4

| PREP TIME: 5 minutes
| COOK TIME: 30 minutes

5 eggs
45 ml chunky tomato sauce
30 g grated Parmesan cheese, plus more for topping
30 ml double cream

1. Combine the eggs and cream in a medium bowl.
2. Mix in the tomato sauce and add the cheese. Spread into 2 greased mini baking dishes.
3. When ready to cook, remove the grill plates and preheat the airfryer baskets for three minutes by activating the automatic preheat key.
4. Place one baking dish in each basket. Select the Match Cook key then set basket 1 to 180°C for 30 minutes, then touch the start key to activate the airfryer.
5. When cooking is complete, remove the baking dishes. Top with extra cheese and serve hot.

Spinach Omelette

SERVES 1

| PREP TIME: 10 minutes
| COOK TIME: 10 minutes

5 ml olive oil
3 eggs
30 g chopped spinach
15 g ricotta cheese
3 g chopped parsley
Salt and ground black pepper, to taste

1. Grease a 18 x13 cm baking dish with olive oil.
2. In a bowl, beat the eggs with a fork and sprinkle with salt and pepper to taste.
3. Add the ricotta, spinach, and parsley. Transfer the mixture into the baking dish.
4. When ready to cook, remove the grill plate from basket 1 then preheat the airfryer basket for three minutes by activating the automatic preheat key.
5. Put the baking dish into basket 1 and set the temperature to 165°C for 10 minutes, then touch the start key to activate the airfryer, until the egg is set.
6. When cooking is complete, serve warm.

Golden Avocado

SERVES 4

| PREP TIME: 5 minutes
| COOK TIME: 12 minutes

cooking spray
1 avocado, pitted, peeled and sliced
Liquid from 1 tin white beans
60 g bread crumbs
½ tsp. salt

1. Mix the bread crumbs and salt in a shallow bowl until well-incorporated.
2. Dip the avocado in the bean liquid, then into the bread crumbs.
3. When ready to cook, remove the grill plate from basket 1 then preheat the airfryer basket for three minutes by activating the automatic preheat key.
4. Put the avocado slices in a single layer into basket 1 and spray with cooking spray. Set the temperature to 180°C for 12 minutes, then touch the start key to activate the airfryer. Halfway through cooking, give the avocado a shake.
5. When cooking is complete, transfer the avocado slices to a plate. Serve warm.

Jacket Potatoes

SERVES 2

| PREP TIME: 5 minutes
| COOK TIME: 30 minutes

2 potatoes
45 g sour cream
15 g butter, softened
15 g mozzarella cheese, shredded
3 g fresh parsley, chopped
1 tsp. chives, minced
Salt and black pepper, to taste

1. Prick the potatoes with a fork.
2. When ready to cook, remove the grill plate from basket 1 then preheat the airfryer basket for three minutes by activating the automatic preheat key.
3. Put the potatoes into basket 1 and set the temperature to 200°C for 30 minutes, then touch the start key to activate the airfryer. Halfway through cooking, carefully flip the potatoes over.
4. When cooking is complete, transfer the potatoes to a plate.
5. Mix together remaining ingredients in a small bowl until well combined.
6. Cut the potatoes from the centre and stuff in the cheese mixture. Serve hot.

English Pumpkin Egg Bake

SERVES 2

| PREP TIME: 10 minutes
| COOK TIME: 10 minutes

15 ml olive oil
225 g pumpkin purée
2 eggs
120 ml milk
250 g flour
30 ml cider vinegar
15 g sugar
10 g baking powder
5 g baking soda
2 g cinnamon powder

1. Grease a 18 x 13-cm baking dish with olive oil.
2. Crack the eggs into a bowl and beat with a whisk. Combine with the flour, milk, cider vinegar, baking powder, sugar, pumpkin purée, cinnamon powder, and baking soda, mixing well.
3. Transfer the mixture into the baking dish.
4. When ready to cook, remove the grill plate from basket 1 then preheat the airfryer basket for three minutes by activating the automatic preheat key.
5. Put the baking dish into basket 1 and set the temperature to 150°C for 10 minutes, then touch the start key to activate the airfryer.
6. When cooking is complete, serve warm.

CHAPTER 2
Vegetable

Caramelised Brussels Sprouts

SERVES 4

| PREP TIME: 10 minutes
| COOK TIME: 20 minutes

20 g butter, melted
450 g Brussels sprouts, trimmed and halved
Salt and black pepper, to taste

1. Mix all the ingredients in a medium bowl and toss to coat well.
2. When ready to cook, remove the grill plate from basket 1 then pre-heat the airfryer basket for three minutes by activating the automatic preheat key.
3. Put the Brussels sprouts into basket 1 and set the temperature to 200°C for 20 minutes, then touch the start key to activate the air-fryer. Halfway through cooking, give the Brussels sprouts a shake.
4. When cooking is complete, transfer the Brussels sprouts to a plate and serve warm.

Parmesan Broccoli with Olives

SERVES 4

| PREP TIME: 15 minutes
| COOK TIME: 19 minutes

30 ml olive oil
900 g broccoli, stemmed and cut into 2.5 cm florets
50 g Kalamata olives, halved and pitted
30 g Parmesan cheese, grated
2 tsps. fresh lemon zest, grated
Salt and ground black pepper, as required

1. Boil the broccoli in a pot for about 4 minutes and drain well.
2. Mix the broccoli, olive oil, salt, and black pepper in a large bowl and toss to coat well.
3. When ready to cook, remove the grill plate from basket 1 then pre-heat the airfryer basket for three minutes by activating the automatic preheat key.
4. Put the broccoli into basket 1 and set the temperature to 200°C for 19 minutes, then touch the start key to activate the airfryer. Halfway through cooking, give the broccoli a shake.
5. When cooking is complete, transfer the broccoli to a plate. Stir in the olives, lemon zest and cheese and serve immediately.

Potato and Egg Salad

SERVES 6

| PREP TIME: 10 minutes
| COOK TIME: 30 minutes

15 ml olive oil
4 Russet potatoes
3 hard-boiled eggs, peeled and chopped
100 g celery, chopped
80 g red onion, chopped
60 ml mayonnaise
Salt, as required
15 ml prepared mustard
¼ tsp. celery salt
¼ tsp. garlic salt

1. Prick the potatoes with a fork and rub with olive oil and salt to taste.
2. When ready to cook, remove the grill plate from basket 1 then pre-heat the airfryer basket for three minutes by activating the automatic preheat key.
3. Put the potatoes into basket 1 and set the temperature to 200°C for 30 minutes, then touch the start key to activate the airfryer. Halfway through cooking, carefully flip the potatoes over.
4. When cooking is complete, transfer the potatoes to a plate and keep aside to cool.
5. Add the remaining ingredients and combine well. Refrigerate for about 2 hours and serve immediately.

Cheesy Mushrooms with Herbs

SERVES 4

| PREP TIME: 10 minutes
| COOK TIME: 7 minutes

30 ml olive oil
170 g button mushrooms, stemmed
12 g Italian dried mixed herbs
20 g mozzarella cheese, grated
20 g cheddar cheese, grated
1 tsp. dried dill
Salt and freshly ground black pepper, to taste

1. Mix the mushrooms, Italian dried mixed herbs, oil, salt and black pepper in a bowl and toss to coat well.
2. When ready to cook, remove the grill plate from basket 1 then pre-heat the airfryer basket for three minutes by activating the automatic preheat key.
3. Put the mushrooms into basket 1 and top with mozzarella cheese and cheddar cheese. Set the temperature to 200°C for 7 minutes, then touch the start key to activate the airfryer.
4. When cooking is complete, transfer the mushrooms to a plate and sprinkle with dried dill to serve.

Garden Green Beans

SERVES 4

| PREP TIME: 10 minutes
| COOK TIME: 12 minutes

cooking spray
450 g green beans, washed and trimmed
5 g butter, melted
15 ml fresh lemon juice
¼ tsp. garlic powder
Salt and freshly ground pepper, to taste

1. Put all the ingredients in a large bowl and mix well.
2. When ready to cook, remove the grill plate from basket 1 then pre-heat the airfryer basket for three minutes by activating the automatic preheat key.
3. Put the green beans into basket 1 and set the temperature to 200°C for 12 minutes, then touch the start key to activate the airfryer. Half-way through cooking, give the green beans a shake.
4. When cooking is complete, transfer the green beans to a plate. Serve warm.

Fresh Parmesan Asparagus

SERVES 3

| PREP TIME: 15 minutes
| COOK TIME: 20 minutes

450 g fresh asparagus, trimmed
15 g Parmesan cheese, grated
15 g butter, melted
1 tsp. garlic powder
Salt and black pepper, to taste

1. Mix the asparagus, Parmesan cheese, butter, garlic powder, salt and black pepper in a bowl and toss to coat well.
2. When ready to cook, remove the grill plate from basket 1 then pre-heat the airfryer basket for three minutes by activating the automatic preheat key.
3. Put the asparagus into basket 1 and set the temperature to 200°C for 20 minutes, then touch the start key to activate the airfryer. Halfway through cooking, flip the asparagus over.
4. When cooking is complete, transfer the asparagus to a plate. Serve warm.

Cauliflower Salad with Sultana

SERVES 4

| PREP TIME: 20 minutes
| COOK TIME: 20 minutes

60 ml olive oil
1 head cauliflower, cut into small florets
40 g golden sultanas
240 g boiling water
40 g pecans, toasted and chopped
8 g fresh mint leaves, chopped
1 tbsp. curry powder
Salt, to taste
For the Dressing:
240 ml mayonnaise
15 ml fresh lemon juice
30 g coconut sugar

1. Mix the cauliflower, pecans, curry powder, oil and salt in a bowl and toss to coat well.
2. When ready to cook, remove the grill plate from basket 1 then preheat the airfryer basket for three minutes by activating the automatic preheat key.
3. Meanwhile, add the sultanas in boiling water in a bowl for about 20 minutes.
4. Put the cauliflower florets into basket 1 and set the temperature to 200°C for 20 minutes, then touch the start key to activate the airfryer. Halfway through cooking, give the cauliflower florets a shake.
5. When cooking is complete, transfer the cauliflower florets to a plate. Drain the sultanas well and mix with the cauliflower florets.
6. Mix all the dressing ingredients in a bowl and pour over the salad. Toss to coat well and serve warm.

Tofu with Orange Sauce

SERVES 4

| PREP TIME: 20 minutes
| COOK TIME: 16 minutes

cooking spray
450 g extra-firm tofu, pressed and cubed
120 ml water
80 ml fresh orange juice
16 g cornflour
2 spring onions (green part), chopped
15 ml tamari
15 ml honey
1 tsp. fresh ginger, minced
1 tsp. orange zest, grated
1 tsp. garlic, minced
¼ tsp. red pepper flakes, crushed

1. Mix the tofu, cornflour and tamari in a medium bowl and toss to coat well.
2. When ready to cook, remove the grill plates and preheat the airfryer baskets for three minutes by activating the automatic preheat key.
3. Place half of the tofu pieces in a single layer in each basket and spray with cooking spray. Select the Match Cook key then set basket 1 to 200°C for 16 minutes, then touch the start key to activate the airfryer.
4. For even browning, carefully turn the tofu pieces halfway through cooking using a silicone spatula.
5. When cooking is complete, transfer the tofu pieces to a plate.
6. Put the remaining ingredients except spring onions in a small pan over medium-high heat and bring to a boil.
7. Pour this sauce over the tofu and garnish with spring onions. Serve warm.

Spiced Aubergine

SERVES 3

| **PREP TIME:** 15 minutes
| **COOK TIME:** 15 minutes

2 medium aubergines, cubed
30 g Parmesan cheese, shredded
30 g butter, melted
15 ml Maggi seasoning sauce
15 ml fresh lemon juice
1 tsp. sumac
1 tsp. onion powder
1 tsp. garlic powder
Salt and ground black pepper, as required

1. Mix the aubergine cubes, melted butter, seasoning sauce and spices in a bowl and toss to coat well.
2. When ready to cook, remove the grill plate from basket 1 then preheat the airfryer basket for three minutes by activating the automatic preheat key.
3. Put the aubergine cubes into basket 1 and set the temperature to 200°C for 15 minutes, then touch the start key to activate the airfryer. Halfway through cooking, give the aubergine cubes a shake.
4. When cooking is complete, transfer the aubergine cubes to a plate and sprinkle with lemon juice and Parmesan cheese. Serve warm.

Veggie Stuffed Bell Peppers

SERVES 6

| **PREP TIME:** 20 minutes
| **COOK TIME:** 25 minutes

1 potato, peeled and finely chopped
1 carrot, peeled and finely chopped
120 g fresh peas, shelled
6 large bell peppers, tops and seeds removed
40 g cheddar cheese, grated
2 garlic cloves, minced
Salt and black pepper, to taste

1. Mix potato, carrot, peas, garlic, salt and black pepper in a bowl.
2. Stuff the vegetable mixture in each bell pepper.
3. When ready to cook, remove the grill plates and preheat the airfryer baskets for three minutes by activating the automatic preheat key.
4. Place half of bell peppers in a single layer in each basket. Select the Match Cook key then set basket 1 to 200°C for 25 minutes, then touch the start key to activate the airfryer.
5. When the bell peppers have been cooking for 20 minutes, top with cheddar cheese. Cook for a further 5 minutes, until the cheese is melted.
6. When cooking is complete, transfer the bell peppers to a plate. Serve hot.

Stuffed Okra

SERVES 2

| PREP TIME: 15 minutes
| COOK TIME: 12 minutes

225 g large okras
30 g chickpea flour
15 g coconut, grated freshly
¼ of onion, chopped
1 tsp. garam masala powder
½ tsp. red chilli powder
½ tsp. ground turmeric
½ tsp. ground cumin
Salt, to taste

1. Mix the flour, onion, grated coconut and spices in a bowl and toss to coat well.
2. When ready to cook, remove the grill plate from basket 1 then preheat the airfryer basket for three minutes by activating the automatic preheat key.
3. Stuff the flour mixture into okras and arrange into basket 1 and set the temperature to 200°C for 12 minutes, then touch the start key to activate the airfryer.
4. When cooking is complete, transfer the okras to a plate and serve warm.

Aubergine Salad with Avocado

SERVES 2

| PREP TIME: 15 minutes
| COOK TIME: 15 minutes

30 ml rapeseed oil
1 aubergine, cut into 1-cm-thick slices crosswise
1 avocado, peeled, pitted and chopped
5 ml fresh lemon juice
Salt and ground black pepper, as required
For the Dressing:
15 ml extra-virgin olive oil
15 ml fresh oregano leaves, chopped
15 ml red wine vinegar
15 ml honey
1 tsp. Dijon mustard
1 tsp. fresh lemon zest, grated
Salt and ground black pepper, as required

1. Mix the aubergine, rapeseed oil, salt, and black pepper in a bowl and toss to coat well.
2. When ready to cook, remove the grill plate from basket 1 then preheat the airfryer basket for three minutes by activating the automatic preheat key.
3. Put the aubergines pieces into basket 1 and set the temperature to 200°C for 15 minutes, then touch the start key to activate the airfryer. Halfway through cooking, carefully flip the aubergines pieces over.
4. When cooking is complete, transfer the aubergines to a plate and keep aside to cool.
5. Add the avocado and lemon juice and mix well.
6. Mix all the dressing ingredients in a bowl and pour over the salad. Toss to coat well and serve immediately.

CHAPTER 3
Poultry

Simple Chicken Wings

SERVES 6

| **PREP TIME:** 5 minutes
| **COOK TIME:** 30 minutes

⅛ tsp. salt
900 g chicken wings, tips removed

1. Season the chicken wings with salt to taste.
2. Preheat the basket 1 with the grill plate inserted for three minutes by activating the automatic preheat key.
3. Place the wings into basket 1 and set the temperature to 200°C for 30 minutes then touch the start key to activate the airfryer. Halfway through cooking, flip the chicken wings over.
4. When cooking is complete, transfer the chicken wings to a plate. Serve warm.

Gingered Chicken Drumsticks

SERVES 3

| **PREP TIME:** 10 minutes
| **COOK TIME:** 22 minutes

3 (170 g) chicken drumsticks
60 ml full-fat coconut milk
2 tsps. ground turmeric
2 tsps. fresh ginger, minced
2 tsps. galangal, minced
Salt, to taste

1. Mix the coconut milk, galangal, ginger, and spices in a medium bowl.
2. Add the chicken drumsticks and coat generously with the marinade.
3. Refrigerate to marinate for at least 8 hours.
4. Preheat the basket 1 with the grill plate inserted for three minutes by activating the automatic preheat key.
5. Place the chicken drumsticks into basket 1 and set the temperature to 200°C for 22 minutes then touch the start key to activate the airfryer. Halfway through cooking, flip the chicken drumsticks over.
6. When cooking is complete, transfer the chicken drumsticks to a plate. Serve warm.

Bacon Wrapped Cheese Stuffed Turkey Breasts

SERVES 4

| PREP TIME: 15 minutes
| COOK TIME: 20 minutes

2 (225 g) turkey breast fillets, skinless and boneless, each cut into 2 pieces
4 cheddar cheese slices
4 rashers of bacon
2 g fresh parsley, minced
Salt and black pepper, to taste

1. Make a slit in each turkey piece horizontally and season with salt and black pepper to taste.
2. Insert the cheddar cheese slices into the slits and sprinkle with parsley.
3. Wrap each turkey piece with one rasher of bacon.
4. Preheat the airfryer baskets with the grill plates inserted for three minutes by activating the automatic preheat key.
5. Place 2 turkey pieces into each basket. Select the Match Cook key and set basket 1 to 200°C for 20 minutes and touch the start key to activate. Halfway through cooking, flip the turkey pieces over.
6. When cooking is complete, transfer the turkey pieces to a plate. Serve warm.

Chicken with Broccoli

SERVES 3

| PREP TIME: 20 minutes
| COOK TIME: 20 minutes

20 g butter
450 g boneless, skinless chicken breasts, sliced
180 g small broccoli florets
1½ tbsps. dried parsley, crushed
½ tbsp. garlic powder
½ tbsp. onion powder
¼ tsp. paprika
¼ tsp. red chilli powder

1. Mix the butter, parsley and spices in a small bowl.
2. Coat the chicken slices and broccoli generously with the spice mixture.
3. When ready to cook, remove the grill plate from basket 2 then preheat the airfryer baskets for three minutes by activating the automatic preheat key.
4. Place the marinated chicken slices onto the grill plate in basket 1 and set the temperature to 190°C for 20 minutes. Put the broccoli into basket 2 and set the temperature to 200°C for 15 minutes, then activate the Smart Finish key and touch the start key to activate the airfryer.
5. Halfway through cooking, give both baskets a shake.
6. When cooking is complete, serve the chicken with broccoli.

Crispy Chicken Drumsticks

SERVES 2

| **PREP TIME:** 15 minutes
| **COOK TIME:** 22 minutes

45 g butter, melted
4 (115 g) chicken drumsticks
120 ml buttermilk
50 g panko breadcrumbs
60 g plain flour
¼ tsp. baking powder
¼ tsp. dried thyme
¼ tsp. dried oregano

¼ tsp. celery salt
¼ tsp. paprika
¼ tsp. garlic powder
¼ tsp. ground ginger
¼ tsp. cayenne pepper
Salt and ground black pepper, as required

1. Put the chicken drumsticks and buttermilk in a resealable plastic bag.
2. Seal the bag tightly and refrigerate for about 3 hours.
3. Mix the flour, breadcrumbs, baking powder, herbs and spices in a small bowl.
4. Remove the chicken drumsticks from bag and coat the chicken drumsticks evenly with the seasoned flour mixture.
5. Preheat the basket 1 with the grill plate inserted for three minutes by activating the automatic preheat key.
6. Place the chicken drumsticks into basket 1 and set the temperature to 200°C for 22 minutes then touch the start key to activate the airfryer. Halfway through cooking, flip the chicken drumsticks over.
7. When cooking is complete, transfer the chicken drumsticks to a plate. Serve warm.

Crispy Chicken Tenders

SERVES 3

| **PREP TIME:** 20 minutes
| **COOK TIME:** 24 minutes

2 (170 g) boneless, skinless chicken breasts, pounded into 1-cm thickness and cut into tenders
2 large eggs
180 g panko breadcrumbs
180 ml buttermilk
60 g plain flour

30 g Parmesan cheese, finely grated
7 ml Worcestershire sauce, divided
½ tsp. smoked paprika, divided
Salt and ground black pepper, as required

1. Mix the buttermilk, ¾ tsp. of Worcestershire sauce, ¼ tsp. of paprika, salt and black pepper in a small bowl.
2. Combine the flour, remaining paprika, salt and black pepper in another bowl.
3. Whisk the egg and remaining Worcestershire sauce in a third bowl.
4. Mix the panko breadcrumbs and Parmesan cheese in a fourth bowl.
5. Place the chicken tenders into the buttermilk mixture and refrigerate overnight.
6. Remove the chicken tenders from the buttermilk mixture and dredge into the flour mixture.
7. Dip into the egg and coat evenly with the breadcrumb mixture.
8. Preheat the airfryer baskets with the grill plates inserted for three minutes by activating the automatic preheat key.
9. Place half of the chicken tenders in a single layer in each basket. Select the Match Cook key and set basket 1 to 200°C for 24 minutes and touch the start key to activate.
10. Halfway through cooking, flip the chicken tenders over.
11. When cooking is complete, transfer the chicken tenders to a plate. Serve warm.

Roasted Chicken with Potatoes

SERVES 2

| PREP TIME: 15 minutes
| COOK TIME: 40 minutes

15 ml olive oil
half of whole chicken (about 1 kg)
225 g small potatoes
Salt and black pepper, as required

1. Season the chicken and potatoes with salt and black pepper to taste and drizzle with olive oil.
2. When ready to cook, remove the grill plate from basket 2 then preheat the airfryer baskets for three minutes by activating the automatic preheat key.
3. Place the chicken onto the grill plate in basket 1 and set the temperature to 200°C for 40 minutes. Put the potatoes into basket 2 and set the temperature to 200°C for 30 minutes, then activate the Smart Finish key and touch the start key to activate the airfryer. Halfway through cooking, flip the chicken over and give the potatoes a shake.
4. When cooking is complete, serve the chicken hot with potatoes.

Parmesan Chicken Cutlets with Mushroom

SERVES 4

| PREP TIME: 15 minutes
| COOK TIME: 30 minutes

2 large eggs
4 (170 g) (0.5-cm thick) skinless, boneless chicken cutlets
150 g panko breadcrumbs
80 g plain flour
30 g Parmesan cheese, grated
1 tbsp. mustard powder
Salt and black pepper, to taste
225 g chestnut mushrooms, halved
2 garlic cloves, finely chopped
30 ml rice vinegar
30 ml maple syrup
30 ml soy sauce

1. Place the flour in a shallow bowl and whisk the eggs in a second bowl.
2. Mix the breadcrumbs, cheese, mustard powder, salt and pepper in a third bowl.
3. Season the chicken with salt and black pepper to taste and coat the chicken with flour.
4. Dip the chicken into whisked eggs and finally dredge into the breadcrumb mixture.
5. When ready to cook, remove the grill plate from basket 2 then preheat the airfryer baskets for three minutes by activating the automatic preheat key.
6. Meanwhile, mix soy sauce, maple syrup, vinegar and garlic in a bowl.
7. Place the chicken cutlets onto the grill plate in basket 1 and set the temperature to 200°C for 30 minutes. Put the mushrooms into basket 2 and set the temperature to 200°C for 15 minutes, then activate the Smart Finish key and touch the start key to activate the airfryer.
8. With 8 minutes remaining, flip the chicken over and spread the soy sauce mixture over the mushrooms. Cook for a further 8 minutes.
9. When cooking is complete, serve the chicken cutlets with mushrooms.

Duck Breast with Cherry Tomato

SERVES 2

| PREP TIME: 15 minutes
| COOK TIME: 20 minutes

2 g fresh thyme, chopped
1 (300 g) duck breast
4 cherry tomatoes
40 g black olives
15 ml olive oil
5 ml mustard
240 ml beer
Salt and freshly ground black pepper, to taste
15 ml balsamic vinegar

1. Mix the olive oil, mustard, thyme, beer, salt and black pepper in a bowl.
2. Add the duck breast and coat generously with this marinade.
3. Cover the duck breast with foil paper and refrigerate for about 4 hours.
4. When ready to cook, remove the grill plate from basket 2 then preheat the airfryer baskets for three minutes by activating the automatic preheat key.
5. Place the duck breast onto the grill plate in basket 1 and set the temperature to 200°C for 25 minutes. Put the tomatoes into basket 2 and set the temperature to 200°C for 15 minutes, then activate the Smart Finish key and touch the start key to activate the airfryer. Halfway through cooking, flip the duck breast and cherry tomatoes over.
6. When cooking is complete, transfer the duck breast and tomatoes to a plate. Drizzle with vinegar and serve topped with olives.

Sweet Chicken Kebabs

SERVES 3

| PREP TIME: 20 minutes
| COOK TIME: 15 minutes

450 g chicken tenders
60 ml sesame oil
120 ml pineapple juice
120 ml soy sauce
4 spring onions, chopped
8 g sesame seeds, toasted
Wooden skewers, pres oaked
6 g fresh ginger, finely grated
4 garlic cloves, minced
A pinch of black pepper

1. Mix the garlic, scallion, ginger, pineapple juice, soy sauce, oil, sesame seeds, and black pepper in a large baking dish.
2. Thread the chicken tenders onto pre-soaked wooden skewers.
3. Coat the skewers generously with this marinade and refrigerate for about 2 hours.
4. Preheat the airfryer baskets with the grill plates inserted for three minutes by activating the automatic preheat key.
5. Place half of the skewers in a single layer into each basket. Select the Match Cook key and set basket 1 to 190°C for 15 minutes and touch the start key to activate. Halfway through cooking, flip the skewers over.
6. When cooking is complete, transfer the skewers to a plate. Serve warm.

Cheese Stuffed Chicken Breast

SERVES 4

| PREP TIME: 15 minutes
| COOK TIME: 24 minutes

2 (225 g) chicken fillets, skinless and boneless, each cut into 2 pieces
4 brie cheese slices
4 cured ham slices
3 g chive, minced
Salt and black pepper, to taste

1. Make a slit in each chicken piece horizontally and season with the salt and black pepper.
2. Insert the cheese slices in the slits and sprinkle with chives. Wrap each chicken piece with one ham slice.
3. Preheat the airfryer baskets with the grill plates inserted for three minutes by activating the automatic preheat key.
4. Carefully place 2 chicken pieces into each basket. Select the Match Cook key and set basket 1 to 190°C for 24 minutes and touch the start key to activate. Halfway through cooking, flip the chicken pieces over.
5. When cooking is complete, transfer the chicken pieces to a plate. Serve hot.

Herbed Turkey Breast

SERVES 3

| PREP TIME: 15 minutes
| COOK TIME: 40 minutes

15 ml olive oil
1 (1.1 kg) bone-in, skin-on turkey breast
1 tsp. dried rosemary, crushed
1 tsp. dried thyme, crushed
½ tsp. dried sage, crushed
½ tsp. garlic powder
½ tsp. dark brown sugar
½ tsp. paprika

1. Mix the herbs, brown sugar, and spices in a small bowl.
2. Drizzle the turkey breast with olive oil and season with the herb mixture.
3. Preheat the basket 1 with the grill plate inserted for three minutes by activating the automatic preheat key.
4. Place the turkey breast into basket 1 and set the temperature to 190°C for 40 minutes then touch the start key to activate the airfryer. Halfway through cooking, flip the turkey breast over.
5. When cooking is complete, transfer the turkey breast to a plate and cut into desired size slices to serve.

CHAPTER 4
Pork

Baked Chorizo Scotch Eggs

MAKES 4 EGGS

| **PREP TIME:** 5 minutes
| **COOK TIME:** 17 minutes

Cooking spray
450 g Mexican chorizo or other seasoned sausage meat
4 soft-boiled eggs plus 1 raw egg
100 g panko bread crumbs
50 g plain flour
15 ml water

1. Divide the chorizo into 4 equal portions. Flatten each portion into a disc. Place a soft-boiled egg in the centre of each disc. Wrap the chorizo around the egg, encasing it completely. Place the encased eggs on a plate and chill for at least 30 minutes.
2. Beat the raw egg with 1 tbsp. of water. Place the flour on a small plate and the panko on a second plate. Working with 1 egg at a time, roll the encased egg in the flour, then dip it in the egg mixture. Dredge the egg in the panko and place on a plate. Repeat with the remaining eggs.
3. Preheat the airfryer baskets with the grill plates inserted for three minutes by activating the automatic preheat key.
4. Spray the eggs with cooking spray and place 2 eggs in a single layer in each basket. Select the Match Cook key and set basket 1 to 200°C for 17 minutes and touch the start key to activate. Halfway through cooking, flip the eggs over.
5. When cooking is complete, transfer the eggs to a plate. Serve warm.

Five Spice Pork

SERVES 4

| **PREP TIME:** 15 minutes
| **COOK TIME:** 16 minutes

450 g pork belly
30 ml dark soy sauce
24 g sugar
15 ml Shaoxing (cooking wine)
15 ml hoisin sauce
2 tsps. garlic, minced
2 tsps. ginger, minced
1 tsp. Chinese Five Spice

1. Mix all the ingredients in a medium bowl and place in the Ziplock bag.
2. Seal the bag, shake it well and refrigerate to marinate for about 1 hour.
3. Remove the pork belly from the bag.
4. Preheat the basket 1 with the grill plate inserted for three minutes by activating the automatic preheat key.
5. Place the pork into basket 1 and set the temperature to 190°C for 16 minutes then touch the start key to activate the airfryer. Halfway through cooking, flip the pork over.
6. When cooking is complete, transfer the pork to a plate. Serve hot.

Pork Loin with Red Potatoes

SERVES 5

| PREP TIME: 15 minutes
| COOK TIME: 30 minutes

900 g pork loin
3 large red potatoes, chopped
45 ml olive oil, divided
1 tsp. fresh parsley, chopped
½ tsp. garlic powder
½ tsp. red pepper flakes, crushed
Salt and ground black pepper, as required

1. Rub the pork loin evenly with 22 ml olive oil, parsley, salt, and black pepper.
2. Mix the red potatoes, remaining oil, garlic powder, red pepper flakes, salt, and black pepper in a bowl.
3. When ready to cook, remove the grill plate from basket 2 then preheat the airfryer baskets for three minutes by activating the automatic preheat key.
4. Place the pork loin onto the grill plate in basket 1 and set the temperature to 190°C for 25 minutes. Put the potatoes into basket 2 and set the temperature to 200°C for 30 minutes, then activate the Smart Finish key and touch the start key to activate the airfryer. Halfway through cooking, flip the pork loin over and give the potatoes a shake.
5. When cooking is complete, cut pork loin into desired size slices and serve alongside potatoes.

Orange Pork Tenderloin

SERVES 3-4

| PREP TIME: 15 minutes
| COOK TIME: 20 minutes

450 g pork tenderloin
120 ml orange juice
60 ml white wine
30 g coconut sugar
10 g Dijon mustard
5 g cornflour

Zest of 1 orange
½ tsp. soy sauce
2 tsps. grated fresh ginger
Salt and freshly ground black pepper, to taste
Oranges, halved, for garnish
Fresh parsley, for garnish

1. Combine the coconut sugar, cornflour, Dijon mustard, orange juice, soy sauce, ginger, white wine and orange zest in a small saucepan and bring the mixture to a boil on the hob.
2. Lower the heat and simmer while you cook the pork tenderloin or until the sauce has thickened.
3. Season the pork tenderloin with salt and freshly ground black pepper.
4. Preheat the basket 1 with the grill plate inserted for three minutes by activating the automatic preheat key.
5. Place the tenderloin into basket 1 and set the temperature to 190°C for 20 minutes then touch the start key to activate the airfryer. Halfway through cooking, flip the tenderloin over.
6. When cooking is complete, transfer the tenderloin to a cutting board and let it rest for 5 minutes. Slice the pork at a slight angle and serve immediately with orange halves and fresh parsley.

Easy Devils on Horseback

SERVES 12

| PREP TIME: 5 minutes
| COOK TIME: 12 minutes

24 (about 130 g) petite pitted prunes
8 rashers of middle bacon, cut crosswise into thirds
30 g crumbled blue stilton cheese, divided

1. Halve the prunes lengthwise, but don't cut them all the way through. Place ½ tsp. of cheese in the centre of each prune. Wrap a piece of bacon around each prune and secure the bacon with a toothpick.
2. When ready to cook, remove the grill plates and preheat the airfryer baskets for three minutes by activating the automatic preheat key.
3. Place half of the prunes in a single layer in each basket. Select the Match Cook key then set basket 1 to 200°C for 12 minutes, then touch the start key to activate the airfryer. Halfway through cooking, flip the prunes over.
4. When cooking is complete, transfer the prunes to a plate. Serve warm.

Cheese Crusted Chops

SERVES 6

| PREP TIME: 10 minutes
| COOK TIME: 18 minutes

Cooking spray
¼ tsp. pepper
½ tsp. salt
6 thick boneless pork chops
80 g pork rind crumbs
2 beaten eggs
30 g grated Parmesan cheese
¼ tsp. chilli powder
½ tsp. onion powder
1 tsp. smoked paprika

1. Rub the pepper and salt on both sides of pork chops.
2. In a food processor, pulse pork rinds into crumbs. Mix the crumbs with chilli powder, onion powder, and paprika in a bowl.
3. Beat the eggs in another bowl.
4. Dip the pork chops into eggs then into pork rind crumb mixture.
5. Preheat the airfryer baskets with the grill plates inserted for three minutes by activating the automatic preheat key.
6. Place 3 pork chops in a single layer in each basket and spritz with cooking spray. Select the Match Cook key and set basket 1 to 190°C for 18 minutes and touch the start key to activate. Halfway through cooking, flip the pork chops over.
7. When cooking is complete, transfer the pork chops to a plate. Serve garnished with the Parmesan cheese.

Tasty Pork Loin Back Ribs

SERVES 2

PREP TIME: 5 minutes **COOK TIME:** 30 minutes	2 tsps. red pepper flakes 2 pork loin back ribs ¾ tsp. ground ginger 3 cloves minced garlic Salt and ground black pepper, to taste

1. Combine the red pepper flakes, ginger, garlic, salt and pepper in a bowl, making sure to mix well. Massage the mixture into the pork loin back ribs.
2. Preheat the basket 1 with the grill plate inserted for three minutes by activating the automatic preheat key.
3. Place pork loin ribs into basket 1 and set the temperature to 190°C for 30 minutes then touch the start key to activate the airfryer. Halfway through cooking, flip the pork loin ribs over.
4. When cooking is complete, transfer the pork loin ribs to a plate. Serve warm.

Tomato Stuffed Pork Roll

SERVES 4

PREP TIME: 20 minutes **COOK TIME:** 18 minutes	7 ml olive oil 4 (170 g) pork cutlets, pounded slightly 40 g sun-dried tomatoes, chopped finely 1 scallion, chopped 8 g fresh parsley, chopped 2 tsps. paprika Salt and freshly ground black pepper, to taste

1. Mix the scallion, tomatoes, parsley, salt and black pepper in a bowl.
2. Coat each cutlet with tomato mixture and roll up the cutlet, securing with cocktail sticks.
3. Coat the rolls with olive oil and rub with paprika, salt and black pepper.
4. Preheat the airfryer baskets with the grill plates inserted for three minutes by activating the automatic preheat key.
5. Place 2 rolls in a single layer in each basket. Select the Match Cook key and set basket 1 to 190°C for 18 minutes and touch the start key to activate. Halfway through cooking, flip the rolls over.
6. When cooking is complete, transfer the rolls to a plate and serve warm.

Teriyaki Pork and Mushroom Rolls

SERVES 6

PREP TIME: 10 minutes **COOK TIME:** 17 minutes	6 (110 g) pork belly slices 170 g Enoki mushrooms 60 ml soy sauce 60 ml mirin 50 g brown sugar 5-cm ginger, chopped 3 g almond flour

1. Mix the brown sugar, mirin, soy sauce, almond flour and ginger together until brown sugar dissolves.
2. Take the pork belly slices and wrap around a bundle of mushrooms. Brush each roll with teriyaki sauce. Chill for half an hour.
3. Preheat the airfryer baskets with the grill plates inserted for three minutes by activating the automatic preheat key.
4. Place 3 rolls in a single layer in each basket. Select the Match Cook key and set basket 1 to 190°C for 17 minutes and touch the start key to activate. Halfway through cooking, flip the rolls over.
5. When cooking is complete, transfer the rolls to a plate. Serve warm.

Chinese Pork Meatballs with Brussels Sprouts

SERVES 3

| PREP TIME: 15 minutes
| COOK TIME: 22 minutes

For the Meatballs:
7 ml olive oil
170 g minced pork
1 egg, beaten
30 g cornflour
7 ml light soy sauce
5 ml oyster sauce
2 ml sesame oil
¼ tsp. five spice powder
¼ tsp. honey
For the Brussels Sprouts:
300 g Brussels sprouts, trimmed and halved lengthwise
15 ml maple syrup
15 ml balsamic vinegar
Salt, as required

1. Mix all the ingredients for Brussels Sprouts in a bowl and toss to coat well.
2. Mix all the ingredients for the meatballs except cornflour and oil in another bowl until well combined.
3. Shape the pork mixture into equal-sized balls and place the cornflour in a shallow dish.
4. Roll the meatballs evenly into cornflour mixture.
5. When ready to cook, remove the grill plate from basket 1, then preheat the airfryer baskets for three minutes by activating the automatic preheat key.
6. Transfer the Brussels Sprouts into basket 1, set the temperature to 200°C and for 22 minutes then carefully place the meatballs onto the grill plate in basket 2, set the temperature to 190°C and for 16 minutes.
7. Select the Smart Finish key then touch the start key to activate the airfryer. Halfway through cooking, give the Brussels Sprouts a shake and flip the meatballs over.
8. When cooking is complete, serve the meatballs hot with Brussels Sprouts.

Pork and Tomato Sala

SERVES 2

| PREP TIME: 20 minutes
| COOK TIME: 16 minutes

225 g pork neck
1 ripe tomato, thickly sliced
1 red onion, sliced
1 bunch fresh basil leaves
1 scallion, chopped
15 ml fish sauce
15 ml soy sauce
7 ml oyster sauce

1. Mix all the sauces in a bowl and spread over the pork neck. Refrigerate for about 3 hours.
2. Preheat the basket 1 with the grill plate inserted for three minutes by activating the automatic preheat key.
3. Place the pork neck into basket 1 and set the temperature to 190°C for 16 minutes then touch the start key to activate the airfryer. Halfway through cooking, flip the pork neck over.
4. When cooking is complete, transfer the pork neck to a plate. Cut into desired size slices and keep aside.
5. Mix the rest of the ingredients in a bowl and top with the pork slices to serve.

Herbed Pork Burgers

SERVES 8

| PREP TIME: 15 minutes
| COOK TIME: 16 minutes

2 small onions, chopped
600 g minced pork
8 burger buns
60 g cheddar cheese, grated
2 g fresh basil, chopped
10 g mustard
10 g garlic puree
10 g tomato puree
2 tsps. dried mixed herbs, crushed
Salt and freshly ground black pepper, to taste

1. Mix all the ingredients in a large bowl except the cheese and buns.
2. Make 8 equal-sized patties from the pork mixture.
3. Preheat the airfryer baskets with the grill plates inserted for three minutes by activating the automatic preheat key.
4. Place 4 patties in a single layer in each basket. Select the Match Cook key and set basket 1 to 190°C for 16 minutes and touch the start key to activate.
5. Halfway through cooking, flip the patties over.
6. When cooking is complete, arrange the patties in buns with cheese to serve.

Vietnamese Pork Chops

SERVES 2

| PREP TIME: 15 minutes
| COOK TIME: 15 minutes

15 ml olive oil
2 pork chops
10 g chopped shallot
9 g chopped garlic
15 ml fish sauce
15 g lemongrass
12 g brown sugar
5 ml soy sauce
1 tsp. ground black pepper

1. Combine the shallot, garlic, fish sauce, lemongrass, soy sauce, brown sugar, olive oil, and pepper in a bowl. Stir to combine well.
2. Add the pork chops and toss to coat well. Place the bowl in the refrigerator to marinate for 2 hours.
3. Preheat the basket 1 with the grill plate inserted for three minutes by activating the automatic preheat key.
4. Remove the pork chops from the bowl and discard the marinade. Place the pork chops into basket 1 and set the temperature to 190°C for 15 minutes then touch the start key to activate the airfryer. Halfway through cooking, flip the pork chops over.
5. When cooking is complete, transfer the pork chops to a plate. Serve warm.

CHAPTER 5
Beef

Simple New York Strip Steak

SERVES 2

| PREP TIME: 10 minutes
| COOK TIME: 16 minutes

5 ml olive oil
1 (270 g) New York strip steak
Crushed red pepper flakes, to taste
Salt and black pepper, to taste

1. Rub the steak generously with red pepper flakes, salt and black pepper and coat with the olive oil.
2. Preheat the basket 1 with the grill plate inserted for three minutes by activating the automatic preheat key.
3. Place the steak into basket 1 and set the temperature to 200°C for 16 minutes then touch the start key to activate the airfryer. Halfway through cooking, flip the steak over.
4. When cooking is complete, transfer the steak to a plate and cut into desired size slices to serve.

Beef with Onion

SERVES 2

| PREP TIME: 15 minutes
| COOK TIME: 18 minutes

15 ml avocado oil
450 g top round beef, cut into 4-cm cubes
30 ml Worcestershire sauce
½ yellow onion, chopped
1 tsp. garlic powder
1 tsp. onion powder
Salt and black pepper, to taste

1. Mix the beef, onion, Worcestershire sauce, avocado oil and spices in a bowl.
2. Preheat the basket 1 with the grill plate inserted for three minutes by activating the automatic preheat key.
3. Place the beef mixture into basket 1 and set the temperature to 200°C for 18 minutes then touch the start key to activate the airfryer. Halfway through cooking, give the beef mixture a shake.
4. When cooking is complete, transfer the beef mixture to a plate and cut the beef into desired size slices to serve.

Tasty Beef Stuffed Bell Peppers

SERVES 4

| PREP TIME: 20 minutes
| COOK TIME: 30 minutes

5 ml olive oil
450 g lean beef, minced
80 g light Mexican cheese, shredded and divided
80 g jasmine rice, cooked
½ medium onion, chopped
4 bell peppers, tops and seeds removed
2 garlic cloves, minced
1 tsp. dried basil, crushed
1 tsp. garlic salt
½ tsp. red chilli powder
225 g tomato sauce, divided
10 ml Worcestershire sauce
Ground black pepper, as required

1. Heat the olive oil in a medium frying pan over medium heat and add the onion and garlic.
2. Sauté for 5 minutes and add the minced beef, basil and spices.
3. Cook for about 10 minutes and drain off the excess grease from frying pan.
4. Stir in the rice, half of the cheese, ⅔ of the tomato sauce and Worcestershire sauce and combine well.
5. Stuff the beef mixture in each bell pepper.
6. When ready to cook, remove the grill plate from basket 1 then preheat the airfryer basket for three minutes by activating the automatic preheat key.
7. Put the bell peppers into basket 1 and set the temperature to 200°C for 15 minutes, then touch the start key to activate the airfryer. Halfway through cooking, top with the remaining tomato sauce and cheese.
8. When cooking is complete, transfer the bell peppers to a plate. Serve warm.

Homemade Beef Burgers

SERVES 6

| PREP TIME: 20 minutes
| COOK TIME: 16 minutes

cooking spray
900 g minced beef
90 ml tomato ketchup
12 cheddar cheese slices
12 burger buns
Salt and black pepper, to taste

1. Mix the beef, salt and black pepper in a bowl.
2. Make small equal-sized patties from the beef mixture.
3. Preheat the airfryer baskets with the grill plates inserted for three minutes by activating the automatic preheat key.
4. Place half of patties in a single layer in each basket and spray with cooking spray. Select the Match Cook key and set basket 1 to 200°C for 16 minutes and touch the start key to activate.
5. For even browning, carefully turn the patties halfway through cooking using a silicone spatula.
6. When cooking is complete, transfer the patties to a plate. Top each patty with 1 cheese slice. Arrange the patties between buns and drizzle with ketchup. Serve hot.

Beef Loin with Thyme and Parsley

SERVES 4

| PREP TIME: 5 minutes
| COOK TIME: 15 minutes

15 g butter, melted
450 g beef loin
1 tsp. garlic salt
¼ tsp. dried thyme
¼ tsp. dried parsley

1. In a bowl, combine the melted butter, thyme, parsley and garlic salt.
2. Cut the beef loin into slices and generously apply the seasoned butter with a brush.
3. Preheat the basket 1 with the grill plate inserted for three minutes by activating the automatic preheat key.
4. Place the beef slices into basket 1 and set the temperature to 200°C for 15 minutes then touch the start key to activate the airfryer. Halfway through cooking, flip the beef over.
5. When cooking is complete, transfer the beef to a plate. Serve warm.

Italian Beef Meatballs

SERVES 6

| PREP TIME: 10 minutes
| COOK TIME: 16 minutes

5 ml vegetable oil
2 large eggs
900 g minced beef
150 g panko breadcrumbs
15 g fresh parsley, chopped
30 g Parmesan cheese, grated
1 small garlic clove, chopped
1 tsp. dried oregano
Salt and black pepper, to taste

1. Mix the beef with all other ingredients in a large bowl until well combined. Make equal-sized balls from the mixture.
2. Preheat the airfryer baskets with the grill plates inserted for three minutes by activating the automatic preheat key.
3. Place half of meatballs in a single layer into each basket. Select the Match Cook key and set basket 1 to 180°C for 16 minutes and touch the start key to activate.
4. Halfway through cooking, flip the meatballs over.
5. When cooking is complete, transfer the meatballs to a plate. Serve warm.

Beef Cheeseburger Egg Rolls

MAKES 6 EGG ROLLS

| PREP TIME: 15 minutes
| COOK TIME: 10 minutes

cooking spray
225 g raw lean beef, minced
60 g chopped onion
60 g chopped bell pepper
21 g shredded Cheddar cheese
6 chopped dill gherkin slices
45 g cream cheese
¼ tsp. onion powder
¼ tsp. garlic powder
1 tbsp. yellow mustard
6 egg roll wrappers

1. In a frying pan, add the beef, bell pepper, onion, onion powder, and garlic powder. Stir and crumble the beef until fully cooked, and vegetables are soft.
2. Turn off the heat and add the cream cheese, mustard, and Cheddar cheese, stirring until melted.
3. Pour the beef mixture into a bowl and fold in gherkins.
4. Lay out egg wrappers and divide the beef mixture into each one. Moisten egg roll wrapper edges with water. Fold sides to the middle and seal with water. Repeat with all other egg rolls.
5. When ready to cook, remove the grill plates and preheat the airfryer baskets for three minutes by activating the automatic preheat key.
6. Place half of the rolls in a single layer in each basket and spray with cooking spray. Select the Match Cook key then set basket 1 to 200°C for 10 minutes, then touch the start key to activate the airfryer.
7. When cooking is complete, transfer the rolls to a plate. Serve hot.

Spicy Beef Roast with Jalapeño

SERVES 8

| PREP TIME: 10 minutes
| COOK TIME: 40 minutes

30 ml extra-virgin olive oil
900 g roast beef, at room temperature
2 jalapeño peppers, thinly sliced
1 tsp. sea salt flakes
1 tsp. black pepper, preferably freshly ground
1 tsp. smoked paprika
A few dashes of liquid smoke

1. Pat the roast dry with kitchen towels. Rub with olive oil and all seasonings along with liquid smoke.
2. Preheat the basket 1 with the grill plate inserted for three minutes by activating the automatic preheat key.
3. Place the roast into basket 1 and set the temperature to 200°C for 40 minutes then touch the start key to activate the airfryer. Halfway through cooking, flip the roast over.
4. When cooking is complete, transfer the roast to a plate. Serve sprinkled with sliced jalapeños. Enjoy!

Perfect Skirt Steak

SERVES 4

| PREP TIME: 15 minutes
| COOK TIME: 16 minutes

2 (225 g) skirt steaks
180 ml olive oil
45 ml red wine vinegar
60 g fresh parsley leaves, chopped finely
9 g fresh oregano, chopped finely
12 g fresh mint leaves, chopped finely
3 garlic cloves, minced
1 tbsp. ground cumin
2 tsps. smoked paprika
1 tsp. cayenne pepper
1 tsp. red pepper flakes, crushed
Salt and freshly ground black pepper, to taste

1. Season the steaks with a little salt and black pepper.
2. Mix all the ingredients in a large bowl except the steaks.
3. Place 4 tbsps. of the herb mixture and steaks in a resealable bag and shake well.
4. Refrigerate for about 24 hours and reserve the remaining herb mixture.
5. Keep the steaks at room temperature for 30 minutes.
6. Preheat the basket 1 with the grill plate inserted for three minutes by activating the automatic preheat key.
7. Place the steaks into basket 1 and set the temperature to 200°C for 16 minutes then touch the start key to activate the airfryer. Halfway through cooking, flip the steaks over.
8. When cooking is complete, transfer the steaks to a plate and sprinkle with the remaining herb mixture to serve.

Beef and Veggie Kebabs

SERVES 4

| PREP TIME: 20 minutes
| COOK TIME: 16 minutes

60 ml olive oil
450 g sirloin steak, cut into 2.5 cm chunks
225 g baby Bella mushrooms, stems removed
1 red onion, cut into 2.5 cm pieces
1 large bell pepper, seeded and cut into 2.5 cm pieces
60 ml soy sauce
5 g coconut sugar
1 tbsp. garlic, minced
½ tsp. ground cumin
Salt and black pepper, to taste

1. Mix the soy sauce, oil, garlic, coconut sugar, cumin, salt and black pepper in a large bowl.
2. Coat the steak cubes generously with this marinade and refrigerate to marinate for about 30 minutes.
3. Thread the steak cubes, mushrooms, bell pepper and onion onto metal skewers.
4. Preheat the airfryer baskets with the grill plates inserted for three minutes by activating the automatic preheat key.
5. Place half of the skewers in a single layer in each basket. Select the Match Cook key and set basket 1 to 200°C for 16 minutes and touch the start key to activate. Halfway through cooking, flip the skewers over.
6. When cooking is complete, transfer the skewers to a plate. Serve warm.

Skirt Steak Strips with Veggies

SERVES 4

| PREP TIME: 10 minutes **| COOK TIME:** 17 minutes	60 ml olive oil, divided 1 (340 g) skirt steak, cut into thin strips 225 g fresh mushrooms, quartered 1 onion, cut into half rings 170 g snow peas 30 ml honey 30 ml soy sauce Salt and black pepper, to taste

1. Mix 30 ml oil, soy sauce and honey in a small bowl and coat the steak strips with this marinade.
2. Put the vegetables, remaining oil, salt and black pepper in another bowl and toss well.
3. When ready to cook, remove the grill plate from basket 2 then preheat the airfryer baskets for three minutes by activating the automatic preheat key.
4. Place the steak strips onto the grill plate in basket 1 and set the temperature to 200°C for 17 minutes. Put the vegetables into basket 2 and set the temperature to 200°C for 15 minutes, then activate the Smart Finish key and touch the start key to activate the airfryer. Give both baskets a shake halfway through cooking.
5. When cooking is complete, serve the steak strips with vegetables.

Mozzarella Beef Brisket

SERVES 6

| PREP TIME: 5 minutes **| COOK TIME:** 25 minutes	10 ml olive oil 340 g beef brisket 2 tsps. Italian herbs 200 g Mozzarella cheese, sliced 1 onion, sliced

1. Cut up the brisket into four equal slices and season with the Italian herbs.
2. Drizzle the beef slices with olive oil.
3. Preheat the basket 1 with the grill plate inserted for three minutes by activating the automatic preheat key.
4. Place the beef slices into basket 1 along with the onion and set the temperature to 180°C for 25 minutes then touch the start key to activate the airfryer.
5. With 5 minutes remaining, put a piece of Mozzarella on top of each piece of brisket. Cook for a further 5 minutes, until the cheese is melted.
6. When cooking is complete, transfer the brisket slices to a plate. Serve warm.

Bacon-Wrapped Beef Hot Dog

SERVES 4

| PREP TIME: 5 minutes **| COOK TIME:** 12 minutes	4 rashers of sugar-free bacon 4 beef hot dogs

1. Wrap the hot dog with a rasher of bacon, securing it with a toothpick. Repeat with the other pieces of bacon and hot dogs.
2. Preheat the basket 1 with the grill plate inserted for three minutes by activating the automatic preheat key.
3. Place the wrapped hot dogs into basket 1 and set the temperature to 200°C for 12 minutes then touch the start key to activate the airfryer. Halfway through cooking, flip the wrapped hot dogs over.
4. When cooking is complete, transfer the wrapped hot dogs to a plate. Serve warm.

CHAPTER 6
Fish and Seafood

Crispy Cod Cakes

SERVES 6

| PREP TIME: 20 minutes
| COOK TIME: 12 minutes

450 g cod fillet
1 egg
80 g coconut, grated and divided
1 scallion, finely chopped
6 g fresh parsley, chopped
1 tsp. fresh lime zest, finely grated
1 tsp. red chilli paste
Salt, as required
15 ml fresh lime juice

1. Put the cod fillet, lime zest, egg, chilli paste, salt and lime juice in a food processor and pulse until smooth.
2. Transfer the cod mixture into a large bowl and add the scallion, parsley and 2 tbsps. of coconut.
3. Mix until well combined and make 12 equal-sized round cakes from the mixture.
4. Place the remaining coconut in a shallow bowl and coat the cod cakes with coconut.
5. Preheat the airfryer baskets with the grill plates inserted for three minutes by activating the automatic preheat key.
6. Place half of cod cakes in a single layer in each basket. Select the Match Cook key and set basket 1 to 200°C for 12 minutes and touch the start key to activate. Halfway through cooking, flip the cod cakes over.
7. When cooking is complete, transfer the cod cakes to a plate. Serve warm.

Marinated Salmon Fillets

SERVES 4

| PREP TIME: 10 minutes
| COOK TIME: 15 minutes

Cooking spray
15 ml olive oil
60 ml soy sauce
60 ml rice wine vinegar
4 (170 g) salmon fillets, skin-on
12 g brown sugar
1 tsp. mustard powder
1 tsp. ground ginger
½ tsp. freshly ground black pepper
½ tsp. minced garlic

1. In a small bowl, combine the soy sauce, brown sugar, rice wine vinegar, olive oil, mustard powder, ginger, black pepper and garlic to make a marinade.
2. Place the salmon fillets in a shallow baking dish and pour this marinade over them. Cover the baking dish and marinate for at least 1 hour in the refrigerator, turning the fillets occasionally to keep them coated in the marinade.
3. Preheat the airfryer baskets with the grill plates inserted for three minutes by activating the automatic preheat key.
4. Shake off as much marinade as possible from the fillets and place 2 fillets in a single layer in each basket. Select the Match Cook key and set basket 1 to 200°C for 15 minutes and touch the start key to activate.
5. When cooking is complete, transfer the salmon fillets to a plate. Serve warm.

Simple Salmon

SERVES 2

| PREP TIME: 5 minutes
| COOK TIME: 10 minutes

15 ml olive oil
Salt and black pepper, as required
2 (170 g) salmon fillets

1. Season each salmon fillet with salt and pepper to taste and drizzle with olive oil.
2. Preheat the basket 1 with the grill plate inserted for three minutes by activating the automatic preheat key.
3. Place the salmon fillets into basket 1 and set the temperature to 200°C for 10 minutes then touch the start key to activate the airfryer. Halfway through cooking, flip the salmon fillets over.
4. When cooking is complete, transfer the salmon to a plate. Serve hot.

Classic Fish Fingers

SERVES 4

| PREP TIME: 15 minutes
| COOK TIME: 15 minutes

Cooking spray
2 eggs
120 g whole-wheat panko bread crumbs
4 fish fillets
60 g whole-wheat flour
1 tsp. seasoned salt
½ tbsp. dried parsley flakes

1. Cut the fish fillets lengthwise into "fingers."
2. In a shallow bowl, mix the whole-wheat flour and seasoned salt.
3. In a small bowl, whisk the eggs with 1 tsp. of water.
4. In another shallow bowl, combine the panko bread crumbs and parsley flakes.
5. Coat each fish finger in the seasoned flour, then in the egg mixture, and dredge them in the panko bread crumbs.
6. Preheat the airfryer baskets with the grill plates inserted for three minutes by activating the automatic preheat key.
7. Place half of fish fingers in a single layer into each basket. Select the Match Cook key and set basket 1 to 200°C for 15 minutes and touch the start key to activate. Halfway through cooking, flip the fish fingers over and lightly spray with cooking spray.
8. When cooking is complete, transfer the fish fingers to a plate. Serve warm.

Breaded Hake

SERVES 2

| PREP TIME: 15 minutes
| COOK TIME: 15 minutes

cooking spray
30 ml vegetable oil
4 (170 g) hake fillets
1 egg
115 g breadcrumbs
1 lemon, cut into wedges

1. Whisk the egg in a shallow bowl and mix the breadcrumbs and vegetable oil in another bowl.
2. Dip the hake fillets into the whisked egg and then, dredge in the breadcrumb mixture.
3. Preheat the airfryer baskets with the grill plates inserted for three minutes by activating the automatic preheat key.
4. Place 2 hake fillets in a single layer in each basket. Select the Match Cook key and set basket 1 to 200°C for 15 minutes and touch the start key to activate. Halfway through cooking, flip the hake fillets over and lightly spray with cooking spray.
5. When cooking is complete, transfer the hake fillets to a plate. Serve warm with lemon wedges.

Cheesy Prawns

SERVES 4

| PREP TIME: 20 minutes
| COOK TIME: 12 minutes

30 ml olive oil
900 g prawns, peeled and deveined
150 g Parmesan cheese, grated
4 garlic cloves, minced
30 ml fresh lemon juice
1 tsp. dried basil
½ tsp. dried oregano
1 tsp. onion powder
½ tsp. red pepper flakes, crushed
Ground black pepper, as required

1. Mix the Parmesan cheese, garlic, oil, herbs, and spices in a large bowl and stir in the prawns.
2. When ready to cook, remove the grill plates and preheat the airfryer baskets for three minutes by activating the automatic preheat key.
3. Place half of the prawns in a single layer in each basket. Select the Match Cook key then set basket 1 to 200°C for 12 minutes, then touch the start key to activate the airfryer. Halfway through cooking, give the prawns a shake.
4. When cooking is complete, transfer the prawns to a plate. Drizzle with lemon juice to serve hot.

Maple Glazed Salmon with Carrot

SERVES 2

| PREP TIME: 10 minutes
| COOK TIME: 16 minutes

15 ml olive oil
2 (170 g) salmon fillets
130 g carrots, peeled and cut into large chunks
30 ml maple syrup
15 ml honey
Salt and black pepper, to taste

1. Coat the salmon fillets evenly with maple syrup and season with salt to taste.
2. Mix the carrots, honey, olive oil, salt and black pepper in a bowl and toss to coat well.
3. When ready to cook, remove the grill plate from basket 2 then preheat the airfryer baskets for three minutes by activating the automatic preheat key.
4. Place the salmon fillets onto the grill plate in basket 1 and set the temperature to 200°C for 15 minutes. Put the carrots into basket 2 and set the temperature to 200°C for 16 minutes, then activate the Smart Finish key and touch the start key to activate the airfryer. Halfway through cooking, flip the salmon over and give the carrot a shake.
5. When cooking is complete, serve the salmon fillets with carrots.

Paprika Prawns and Brussels Sprouts

SERVES 2

| PREP TIME: 10 minutes
| COOK TIME: 20 minutes

45 ml olive oil, divided
450 g tiger prawns
450 g Brussels sprouts, trimmed and halved
30 g whole wheat breadcrumbs
30 g Parmesan cheese, shredded
15 ml balsamic vinegar
½ tsp. smoked paprika
Salt and black pepper, to taste

1. Mix the prawns, 30 ml olive oil, paprika and salt to taste in a large bowl until well combined.
2. Mix the Brussels sprouts, vinegar, the remaining 15 ml olive oil, salt, and black pepper in another bowl and toss to coat well.
3. When ready to cook, remove the grill plate from basket 2 then preheat the airfryer baskets for three minutes by activating the automatic preheat key.
4. Place the prawns onto the grill plate in basket 1 and set the temperature to 200°C for 12 minutes. Put the Brussels sprouts into basket 2 and set the temperature to 200°C for 20 minutes, then activate the Smart Finish key and touch the start key to activate the airfryer.
5. With 8 minutes remaining, give the prawns a shake and sprinkle the breadcrumbs and cheese over the Brussels sprouts. Cook for a further 8 minutes.
6. When cooking is complete, serve the prawns with Brussels sprouts.

Herbed Haddock with Cheese Sauce

SERVES 2

| PREP TIME: 10 minutes
| COOK TIME: 12 minutes

120 ml extra-virgin olive oil
2 (170 g) haddock fillets
20 g pine nuts
10 g Parmesan cheese, grated
12 g fresh basil, chopped
Salt and black pepper, to taste

1. Coat the haddock fillets evenly with the oil and season with salt and black pepper to taste.
2. Preheat the basket 1 with the grill plate inserted for three minutes by activating the automatic preheat key.
3. Place the haddock fillets into basket 1 and set the temperature to 200°C for 12 minutes then touch the start key to activate the airfryer. Halfway through cooking, flip the haddock fillets over.
4. Meanwhile, put the remaining ingredients in a food processor and pulse until smooth.
5. When cooking is complete, transfer the haddock fillets to a plate. Top the cheese sauce over the haddock fillets and serve hot.

Spiced Catfish

SERVES 4

| PREP TIME: 10 minutes
| COOK TIME: 15 minutes

15 ml olive oil
4 (170 g) catfish fillets
36 g salt
18 g cornmeal
16 g corn flour
2 tbsps. garlic

1. Mix the catfish fillets with cornmeal, corn flour, garlic and salt in a bowl. Drizzle with olive oil.
2. Preheat the airfryer baskets with the grill plates inserted for three minutes by activating the automatic preheat key.
3. Place 2 catfish fillets in a single layer in each basket. Select the Match Cook key and set basket 1 to 200°C for 15 minutes and touch the start key to activate. Halfway through cooking, flip the catfish fillets over.
4. When cooking is complete, transfer the catfish fillets to a plate. Serve warm.

Sweet and Sour Glazed Cod

SERVES 2

| PREP TIME: 20 minutes
| COOK TIME: 12 minutes

4 (100 g) cod fillets
80 ml honey
80 ml soy sauce
5 ml water
15 ml rice wine vinegar

1. Mix the soy sauce, honey, vinegar and water in a small bowl.
2. Reserve about half of the mixture in another bowl.
3. Stir the cod fillets in the remaining mixture until evenly coated.
4. Cover and refrigerate to marinate for about 3 hours.
5. Preheat the basket 1 with the grill plate inserted for three minutes by activating the automatic preheat key.
6. Place the cod fillets into basket 1 and set the temperature to 200°C for 12 minutes then touch the start key to activate the airfryer. Halfway through cooking, flip the cod fillets over.
7. When cooking is complete, transfer the cod fillets to a plate. Coat with the reserved marinade and serve hot.

Cod and Veggies

SERVES 4

| PREP TIME: 20 minutes
| COOK TIME: 25 minutes

15 ml olive oil
30 g butter, melted
2 (140 g) frozen cod fillets, thawed
70 g carrots, peeled and julienned
70 g red bell peppers, seeded and thinly sliced
70 g fennel bulbs, julienned
15 ml fresh lemon juice
½ tsp. dried tarragon
Salt and ground black pepper, as required

1. Mix the butter, lemon juice, tarragon, salt and black pepper in a large bowl.
2. Add the bell peppers, carrot and fennel bulb and generously coat with the butter mixture.
3. Coat the cod fillets with olive oil and season with salt and black pepper. Top with any remaining sauce from the bowl.
4. When ready to cook, remove the grill plate from basket 2 then preheat the airfryer baskets for three minutes by activating the automatic preheat key.
5. Place the cod fillets onto the grill plate in basket 1 and set the temperature to 200°C for 15 minutes. Put the vegetables into basket 2 and set the temperature to 200°C for 25 minutes, then activate the Smart Finish key and touch the start key to activate the airfryer.
6. When zones have finished cooking, check the cod fillets for doneness. Transfer the cod fillets to a plate and serve with vegetables.

Cajun Salmon Burgers

SERVES 4

| PREP TIME: 10 minutes
| COOK TIME: 15 minutes

Cooking spray
4 (140 g) tins pink salmon in water, any skin and bones removed, drained
2 eggs, beaten
110 g whole-wheat bread crumbs
4 whole-wheat buns
60 ml light mayonnaise
2 tsps. Cajun seasoning
2 tsps. dry mustard

1. In a medium bowl, mix the salmon, eggs, bread crumbs, mayonnaise, Cajun seasoning and dry mustard. Cover with clingfilm and refrigerate for 30 minutes.
2. Shape the salmon mixture into four 1-cm-thick patties about the same size as the buns.
3. Preheat the airfryer baskets with the grill plates inserted for three minutes by activating the automatic preheat key.
4. Place 2 salmon patties in a single layer in each basket. Select the Match Cook key and set basket 1 to 200°C for 15 minutes and touch the start key to activate. Halfway through cooking, flip the patties over and lightly spray with cooking spray.
5. When cooking is complete, transfer the patties to a plate. Serve on whole-wheat buns.

CHAPTER 7
Snack

Cajun Courgette Crisps

SERVES 4

| PREP TIME: 5 minutes
| COOK TIME: 15-16 minutes

Cooking spray
2 large courgettes, cut into 3-mm-thick slices
2 tsps. Cajun seasoning

1. Place the courgette slices in a medium bowl and spray generously with cooking spray.
2. Sprinkle the Cajun seasoning over the courgettes and stir to make sure they are evenly coated with oil and seasoning.
3. When ready to cook, remove the grill plates and preheat the airfryer baskets for three minutes by activating the automatic preheat key.
4. Place half of the slices in a single layer in each basket. Select the Match Cook key then set basket 1 to 200°C for 25 minutes, then touch the start key to activate the airfryer. Halfway through cooking, give the courgette slices a shake.
5. When cooking is complete, transfer the courgette slices to a plate. Serve immediately.

Crispy Prosciutto-Wrapped Asparagus

SERVES 6

| PREP TIME: 5 minutes
| COOK TIME: 12 minutes

Cooking spray
12 asparagus spears, woody ends trimmed
24 pieces thinly sliced prosciutto

1. Wrap each asparagus spear with 2 slices of prosciutto, then repeat this process with the remaining asparagus and prosciutto.
2. When ready to cook, remove the grill plates and preheat the airfryer baskets for three minutes by activating the automatic preheat key.
3. Place 6 bundles in a single layer in each in each basket and spray with cooking spray. Select the Match Cook key then set basket 1 to 200°C for 12 minutes, then touch the start key to activate the airfryer. Halfway through cooking, flip the asparagus bundles over.
4. When cooking is complete, remove the bundles and allow to cool on a wire rack for 5 minutes before serving.

BBQ Pork Ribs

SERVES 2

| PREP TIME: 5 minutes
| COOK TIME: 35 minutes

1 kg individually cut pork spare ribs
12 g dark brown sugar
18 g coarse salt
8 g sweet paprika
1 tsp. poultry seasoning
1 tsp. garlic powder
1 tsp. onion powder
½ tsp. mustard powder
½ tsp. freshly ground black pepper

1. In a large bowl, whisk together the salt, brown sugar, paprika, mustard powder, garlic powder, onion powder, poultry seasoning and pepper. Add the pork ribs and toss. Rub the seasonings into them with your hands until they're fully coated.
2. Preheat the airfryer baskets with the grill plates inserted for three minutes by activating the automatic preheat key.
3. Place half of the pork ribs in each basket, standing up on their ends and leaned up against the wall of the basket and each other. Select the Match Cook key and set basket 1 to 200°C for 35 minutes and touch the start key to activate. Halfway through cooking, flip the pork ribs over.
4. When cooking is complete, transfer the pork ribs to a plate. Serve warm.

Spiced Sweet Potato Chips with Garlic Sour Cream

SERVES 2

| PREP TIME: 10 minutes
| COOK TIME: 15 minutes

30 ml olive oil
2 medium sweet potatoes (about 280 g each), cut into wedges, 1-cm thick and 7-cm long
1½ tsps. smoked paprika
1½ tsps. coarse salt, plus more as needed
1 tsp. chilli powder
½ tsp. ground turmeric
½ tsp. ground cumin
¼ tsp. cayenne pepper
½ tsp. mustard powder
Freshly ground black pepper, to taste
160 ml sour cream
1 garlic clove, grated

1. In a large bowl, combine the oil, cumin, turmeric, paprika, salt, chilli powder, mustard powder and cayenne. Add the sweet potatoes, season with black pepper, and toss to evenly coat.
2. When ready to cook, remove the grill plate from basket 1 then preheat the airfryer basket for three minutes by activating the automatic preheat key.
3. Place the sweet potatoes into basket 1 (save the bowl with the leftover oil and spices), and set the temperature to 200°C for 15 minutes, then touch the start key to activate the airfryer. Halfway through cooking, give the sweet potatoes a shake.
4. Meanwhile, in a small bowl, stir together the sour cream and garlic. Season with salt and black pepper and transfer to a serving dish.
5. When cooking is complete, return the sweet potato wedges to the reserved bowl and toss again while they are hot. Serve the sweet potato wedges hot with the garlic sour cream.

Crispy Pot Stickers

MAKES 30 POT STICKERS

| **PREP TIME:** 10 minutes
| **COOK TIME:** 12 minutes

30 wonton wrappers
50 g finely chopped cabbage
30 g finely chopped red bell pepper
1 egg, beaten
2 spring onions, finely chopped
30 ml cocktail sauce
10 ml low-sodium soy sauce
15 ml water, for brushing the wrappers

1. In a small bowl, combine the cabbage, red pepper, spring onions, egg, cocktail sauce, and soy sauce and mix well.
2. Put about 1 tsp. of the mixture in the centre of each wonton wrapper. Fold the wrapper in half, covering the filling; dampen the edges with water, and seal. You can crimp the edges of the wrapper with your fingers so they look like the pot stickers you get in restaurants. Brush them with water.
3. When ready to cook, remove the grill plates and preheat the airfryer baskets for three minutes by activating the automatic preheat key.
4. Place half of the pot sticker in each basket. Select the Match Cook key then set basket 1 to 180°C for 12 minutes, then touch the start key to activate the airfryer. Cook until the pot stickers are hot and the bottoms are lightly browned.
5. When cooking is complete, serve hot.

Peppery Chicken Meatballs

MAKES 16 MEATBALLS

| **PREP TIME:** 5 minutes
| **COOK TIME:** 18-20 minutes

10 ml olive oil
225 g chicken breast, minced
1 egg white
30 g minced onion
30 g minced red bell pepper
2 vanilla wafers, crushed
½ tsp. dried thyme

1. In a frying pan over medium heat, add the oil, onion and red bell pepper. Cook for about 3 to 5 minutes, until the vegetables are tender.
2. In a medium bowl, mix the cooked vegetables, crushed wafers, egg white, and thyme until well combined.
3. Stir in the chicken, gently but thoroughly, until everything is combined. Form the chicken mixture into 16 meatballs.
4. Preheat the airfryer baskets with the grill plates inserted for three minutes by activating the automatic preheat key.
5. Place 8 meatballs in a single layer into each basket. Select the Match Cook key and set basket 1 to 190°C for 15 minutes and touch the start key to activate. Halfway through cooking, flip the meatballs over.
6. When cooking is complete, transfer the meatballs to a plate. Serve warm.

Apple Crisps

SERVES 2

| PREP TIME: 5 minutes
| COOK TIME: 7 hours

2 Pink Lady apples

1. Core the apples with an apple corer, leaving apple whole. Cut the apples into 3-mm-thick slices.
2. Preheat the airfryer baskets with the grill plates inserted for three minutes by activating the automatic preheat key.
3. Carefully place half of apple slices in a single layer into each basket. Choose the basket 1 and select Dehydrate key, then set temperature to 60°C for 7 hours. Repeat with the basket 2 and touch the start key to activate.
4. When cooking is complete, place the apple slices in a single layer on a wire rack to cool. Apples will become crisper as they cool. Serve immediately.

Spiced Mixed Nuts

SERVES 4

| PREP TIME: 5 minutes
| COOK TIME: 6 minutes

30 ml olive oil
75 g raw cashews
70 g raw whole almonds
55 g raw pecan halves
50 g raw walnut halves
12 g light brown sugar
1 tsp. coarse salt
1 tsp. chopped fresh rosemary leaves
1 tsp. chopped fresh thyme leaves
½ tsp. ground coriander
¼ tsp. onion powder
¼ tsp. freshly ground black pepper
⅛ tsp. garlic powder

1. In a large bowl, combine all the ingredients and toss until the nuts are well coated in the herbs, spices and sugar.
2. When ready to cook, remove the grill plate from basket 1 then preheat the airfryer basket for three minutes by activating the automatic preheat key.
3. Scrape the nuts and seasonings into basket 1 and set the temperature to 180°C for 6 minutes, then touch the start key to activate the airfryer. Halfway through cooking, give the nuts a shake. Cook until golden brown and fragrant.
4. When cooking is complete, transfer the cocktail nuts to a bowl and serve warm.

Chicken Drumsticks with Tortilla Crisps

SERVES 2

| PREP TIME: 5 minutes
| COOK TIME: 25 minutes

15 ml olive oil
4 chicken drumsticks (115 g each)
2 tsps. freshly ground coarse black pepper
1 tsp. baking powder
½ tsp. garlic powder
coarse salt, to taste
1 lemon
2 corn tortillas, sliced the corn tortillas into triangles

1. In a small bowl, stir together the pepper, baking powder and garlic powder.
2. Place the chicken drumsticks on a plate and sprinkle evenly with the baking powder mixture, turning the drumsticks so they're well coated. Let the chicken drumsticks stand in the refrigerator for at least 1 hour or up to overnight.
3. Coat the tortillas pieces with a light brushing of olive oil.
4. When ready to cook, remove the grill plate from basket 2 then preheat the airfryer baskets for three minutes by activating the automatic preheat key.
5. Sprinkle the drumsticks with salt and arrange onto the grill plate in basket 1, standing them bone-end up and leaning against the wall of the basket, and set the temperature to 200°C for 25 minutes. Put the tortillas pieces into basket 2 and set the temperature to 200°C for 6 minutes, then activate the Smart Finish key and touch the start key to activate the airfryer.
6. When cooking is complete, transfer the chicken drumsticks and tortillas pieces to a serving platter.
7. Finely grate the zest of the lemon over the drumsticks while they're hot. Cut the lemon into wedges and serve immediately.

BBQ Bacon Wrapped Prawns and Jalapeño

SERVES 8

| PREP TIME: 20 minutes
| COOK TIME: 15 minutes

24 large prawns, peeled and deveined, about 340 g
24 small pickled jalapeño slices
12 rashers of bacon, cut in half
75 ml barbecue sauce, divided

1. Toss together the prawns and 45 ml barbecue sauce. Let stand for about 15 minutes. Soak 24 wooden toothpicks in water for 10 minutes.
2. Wrap 1 piece bacon around the prawn and jalapeño slice, then secure with a toothpick.
3. When ready to cook, remove the grill plates and preheat the airfryer baskets for three minutes by activating the automatic preheat key.
4. Place half of the prawns in a single layer in each basket. Select the Match Cook key then set basket 1 to 180°C for 15 minutes, then touch the start key to activate the airfryer. Halfway through cooking, flip the prawns over.
5. When cooking is complete, transfer the prawns to a plate. Brush with the remaining barbecue sauce and serve hot.

Prawns Toast

SERVES 4

| **PREP TIME:** 15 minutes
| **COOK TIME:** 7 minutes

8 large raw prawns, peeled and finely chopped
1 egg white
1 medium celery stalk, minced
30 g minced red bell pepper
20 g cornflour
2 garlic cloves, minced
¼ tsp. Chinese five-spice powder
3 slices firm thin-sliced no-sodium whole-wheat bread

1. In a small bowl, stir together the prawns, red bell pepper, celery, egg white, garlic, cornflour, and five-spice powder.
2. Top each slice of bread with one-third of the prawn mixture, spreading it evenly to the edges. With a sharp knife, cut each slice of bread into 4 strips.
3. When ready to cook, remove the grill plates and preheat the airfryer baskets for three minutes by activating the automatic preheat key.
4. Place half of the prawn toasts in each basket. Select the Match Cook key then set basket 1 to 180°C for 7 minutes, then touch the start key to activate the airfryer. Cook until crisp and golden brown.
5. When cooking is complete, serve hot.

Cheesy Hash Brown Bruschetta

SERVES 4

| **PREP TIME:** 5 minutes
| **COOK TIME:** 10 minutes

15 ml olive oil
4 frozen hash brown patties
60 g chopped cherry tomatoes
20 g grated Parmesan cheese
45 g diced fresh Mozzarella
15 ml balsamic vinegar
2 g minced fresh basil

1. Remove the grill plates and preheat the airfryer baskets for three minutes by activating the automatic preheat key.
2. Place 2 hash brown patties in a single layer in each basket. Select the Match Cook key then set basket 1 to 200°C for 10 minutes, then touch the start key to activate the airfryer. Bake until the hash brown patties are crisp, hot, and golden brown.
3. Meanwhile, combine the olive oil, tomatoes, Mozzarella, Parmesan, vinegar, and basil in a small bowl.
4. When cooking is complete, transfer the hash brown patties to a serving plate. Top with the tomato mixture and serve hot.

CHAPTER 8
Dessert

Double Chocolate Muffins

SERVES 12

| **PREP TIME:** 20 minutes
| **COOK TIME:** 16 minutes

170 g self-rising flour
18 g cocoa powder
100 g butter
75 ml milk
70 g milk chocolate, finely chopped
170 g caster sugar
½ tsp. vanilla extract

1. Grease 12 muffin moulds lightly.
2. Mix the flour, sugar, and cocoa powder in a bowl.
3. Stir in the butter, milk, vanilla extract and chopped chocolate and mix until well combined. Transfer the mixture evenly into the muffin moulds.
4. When ready to cook, remove the grill plates and preheat the airfryer baskets for three minutes by activating the automatic preheat key.
5. Place half of the muffin moulds in each basket. Select the Match Cook key then set basket 1 to 180°C for 16 minutes, then touch the start key to activate the airfryer. Bake until toothpick inserted in centre comes out clean.
6. When cooking is complete, serve warm.

Cream Cheese Cupcakes

SERVES 10

| **PREP TIME:** 10 minutes
| **COOK TIME:** 20 minutes

cooking spray
130 g self-rising flour
135 g butter, softened
2 eggs
15 g cream cheese, softened
120 g caster sugar
60 g fresh raspberries
10 ml fresh lemon juice
Pinch of salt

1. Grease 10 silicon cups with cooking spray lightly.
2. Mix the flour, baking powder and salt in a small bowl.
3. Combine the cream cheese, sugar, eggs and butter in another bowl.
4. Mix the flour mixture with the cream cheese mixture and squeeze in the lemon juice.
5. Transfer the mixture into 10 silicon cups and top each cup with 2 raspberries.
6. When ready to cook, remove the grill plates and preheat the airfryer baskets for three minutes by activating the automatic preheat key.
7. Place half of the silicon cups in a single layer in each basket. Select the Match Cook key then set basket 1 to 180°C for 20 minutes, then touch the start key to activate the airfryer. Bake until toothpick inserted in centre comes out clean.
8. When cooking is complete, transfer the cupcakes to a plate and serve to enjoy.

Tasty Lemony Scones

SERVES 10

| PREP TIME: 15 minutes
| COOK TIME: 8 minutes

240 g self-rising flour
100 g cold butter
100 g caster sugar
1 small egg
30 ml fresh lemon juice
1 tsp. fresh lemon zest, grated finely
1 tsp. vanilla extract

1. Grease two 18x13 cm baking dishes lightly.
2. Mix the flour and sugar in a large bowl.
3. Add the cold butter and mix until a coarse crumb is formed.
4. Stir in the egg, lemon zest and lemon juice and mix until a dough is formed.
5. Press the dough into 1-cm thickness onto a floured surface and cut dough into medium-sized scones. Arrange the scones on the baking dishes in a single layer.
6. When ready to cook, remove the grill plates and preheat the airfryer baskets for three minutes by activating the automatic preheat key.
7. Place one baking dish in each basket. Select the Match Cook key then set basket 1 to 180°C for 8 minutes, then touch the start key to activate the airfryer, until golden brown.
8. When cooking is complete, transfer the scones to a plate and serve with tea.

Flavour-Packed Clafoutis

SERVES 4

| PREP TIME: 10 minutes
| COOK TIME: 25 minutes

220 g fresh cherries, pitted
120 ml sour cream
1 egg
15 g butter
45 ml vodka
30 g flour
30 g sugar
Pinch of salt
30 g icing sugar

1. Grease a 18x13 cm baking pan lightly.
2. Mix the cherries and vodka in a bowl.
3. Sift together flour, sugar and salt in another bowl.
4. Gently stir in the sour cream and egg until a smooth dough is formed.
5. Transfer the dough evenly into the greased baking pan and top with the cherry mixture and butter.
6. When ready to cook, remove the grill plate from basket 1 then preheat the airfryer basket for three minutes by activating the automatic preheat key.
7. Place the baking pan into basket 1 and set the temperature to 180°C for 25 minutes, then touch the start key to activate the airfryer.
8. When cooking is complete, dust with icing sugar and serve hot.

Buttered Bread Rolls

SERVES 2

| **PREP TIME:** 10 minutes
| **COOK TIME:** 6 minutes

Cooking spray
30 g unsalted butter, melted
60 g Parmesan cheese, grated
2 bread rolls
½ tsp. garlic bread seasoning mix

1. Cut the bread rolls in slits and stuff cheese in the slits.
2. Top the with butter and garlic bread seasoning mix.
3. When ready to cook, remove the grill plate from basket 1 then preheat the airfryer basket for three minutes by activating the automatic preheat key.
4. Spray basket 1 with cooking spray and place bread rolls in it. Set the temperature to 180°C for 6 minutes, then touch the start key to activate the airfryer. Halfway through cooking, flip the bread rolls over.
5. When cooking is complete, transfer the bread rolls to a plate. Serve warm.

Apple Cake

SERVES 6

| **PREP TIME:** 10 minutes
| **COOK TIME:** 45 minutes

80 ml vegetable oil
120 g plain flour
280 g apples, peeled, cored and chopped
60 g brown sugar
1 egg
2 g baking soda
2 g ground nutmeg
2 g ground cinnamon
¾ tsp. vanilla extract
Salt, to taste

1. Grease a 18x13 cm baking pan lightly.
2. Mix the flour, sugar, spices, baking soda and salt in a bowl until well combined.
3. Whisk the egg with oil and vanilla extract in another bowl.
4. Stir in the flour mixture and gently fold in the apples.
5. Pour this mixture into the baking pan and cover with the foil paper.
6. When ready to cook, remove the grill plate from basket 1 then preheat the airfryer basket for three minutes by activating the automatic preheat key.
7. Place the baking pan into basket 1 and set the temperature to 180°C for 45 minutes, then touch the start key to activate the airfryer.
8. After 40 minutes, remove the foil and cook for a further 5 minutes. Bake until toothpick inserted in centre comes out clean.
9. When cooking is complete, allow to cool completely and cut into slices to serve.

Simple Chocolate Doughnuts

SERVES 8

| PREP TIME: 5 minutes
| COOK TIME: 10 minutes

Cooking oil
1 (225 g) cookies dough
Chocolate sauce, for drizzling

1. Separate the cookies dough into 8 biscuits and place them on a flat work surface. Use a small circle cookie cutter or a biscuit cutter to cut a hole in the centre of each biscuit. You can also cut the holes using a knife.
2. When ready to cook, remove the grill plates and preheat the airfryer baskets for three minutes by activating the automatic preheat key.
3. Spray the doughnuts with cooking oil and place half of doughnuts in each basket. Select the Match Cook key then set basket 1 to 190°C for 10 minutes, then touch the start key to activate the airfryer. Halfway through cooking, flip the doughnuts over.
4. When cooking is complete, transfer the doughnuts to a plate. Drizzle the chocolate sauce over the doughnuts and serve warm.

Pineapple Sticks with Coconut

SERVES 4

| PREP TIME: 5 minutes
| COOK TIME: 10 minutes

½ fresh pineapple, cut into sticks
20 g desiccated coconut

1. Coat the pineapple sticks evenly with the desiccated coconut.
2. When ready to cook, remove the grill plate from basket 1 then preheat the airfryer basket for three minutes by activating the automatic preheat key.
3. Put the pineapple sticks into basket 1 and set the temperature to 200°C for 10 minutes, then touch the start key to activate the airfryer. Halfway through cooking, flip the pineapple sticks over.
4. When cooking is complete, transfer the pineapple sticks to a plate. Serve warm.

Homemade Apple Crumble

SERVES 4

| PREP TIME: 10 minutes
| COOK TIME: 25 minutes

1 (400 g) tin apple pie
90 g caster sugar
90 g self-rising flour
30 g butter, softened
Pinch of salt

1. Grease a 18x13 cm baking dish.
2. Mix all the ingredients except the apple pie in a bowl until a crumbly mixture is formed.
3. Arrange the apple pie in the baking dish and top with the mixture.
4. When ready to cook, remove the grill plate from basket 1 then preheat the airfryer basket for three minutes by activating the automatic preheat key.
5. Place the baking dish in basket 1 and set the temperature to 160°C for 25 minutes, then touch the start key to activate the airfryer.
6. When cooking is complete, transfer the apple crumble to a plate. Serve immediately.

Orange Chocolate Pudding

SERVES 4

| PREP TIME: 10 minutes
| COOK TIME: 12 minutes

110 g butter
110 g dark chocolate, chopped
2 medium eggs
60 ml fresh orange juice
50 g caster sugar
4 g fresh orange rind, grated finely
16 g self-rising flour

1. Grease four 7-cm ramekins lightly.
2. Microwave the butter and chocolate in a bowl on high for about 2 minutes.
3. Add the sugar, eggs, orange rind and juice and mix until well combined.
4. Stir in the flour and combine well. Divide this mixture evenly into the ramekins.
5. When ready to cook, remove the grill plates and preheat the airfryer baskets for three minutes by activating the automatic preheat key.
6. Place 2 ramekins in each basket. Select the Match Cook key then set basket 1 to 180°C for 12 minutes, then touch the start key to activate the airfryer.
7. When cooking is complete, dish out and serve chilled.

Eggnog Bread

SERVES 6

| PREP TIME: 10 minutes
| COOK TIME: 18 minutes

Cooking spray
120 g flour, plus more for dusting
120 ml eggnog
50 g sugar
40 g chopped candied fruit (cherries, pineapple, or mixed fruits)
30 g pecans
1 egg yolk
20 g butter, melted
5 g baking powder
¼ tsp. salt
¼ tsp. nutmeg

1. In a medium bowl, stir together the flour, sugar, baking powder, salt and nutmeg.
2. Add the eggnog, egg yolk, and butter. Mix well but do not beat.
3. Stir in nuts and candied fruit.
4. Spray a 18x13 cm baking pan with cooking spray and dust with flour. Spread the batter into the prepared baking pan.
5. When ready to cook, remove the grill plate from basket 1 then preheat the airfryer basket for three minutes by activating the automatic preheat key.
6. Place the baking pan into basket 1 and set the temperature to 180°C for 18 minutes, then touch the start key to activate the airfryer. Bake until top is dark golden brown and bread starts to pull away from sides of pan.
7. When cooking is complete, serve immediately.

Classic Butter Biscuits

SERVES 8

| PREP TIME: 10 minutes
| COOK TIME: 10 minutes

115 g unsalted butter
120 g plain flour
1 g baking powder
35 g icing sugar

1. Grease a 18x13 cm baking dish lightly.
2. Mix the butter, icing sugar, flour and baking powder in a large bowl.
3. Combine well until a dough is formed and transfer into the piping bag fitted with a fluted nozzle. Pipe the dough onto the baking dish.
4. When ready to cook, remove the grill plate from basket 1 then preheat the airfryer basket for three minutes by activating the automatic preheat key.
5. Place the baking dish into basket 1 and set the temperature to 170°C for 10 minutes, then touch the start key to activate the airfryer. Bake until golden brown.
6. When cooking is complete, serve warm.

Appendix 1: Tower Vortx Duo Basket Pre-Set Menu Table

The table below shows the pre-set times and cooking temperatures for each of the unit's 12 auto-cook menus.

PRE-SET FUNCTIONS	DEFAULT TIME	DEFAULT TEMP (°C)
PRE-HEAT	3 minsw	180°C
FRIES	18 mins	200°C
MEAT	12 mins	200°C
DRUMSTICKS	20 mins	200°C
STEAK	12 mins	180°C
CAKE	25 mins	160°C
PRAWN	8 mins	180°C
FISH	10 mins	180°C
PIZZA	20 mins	180°C
VEGETABLES	10 mins	160°C
RE-HEAT	15 mins	150°C
DEHYDRATE	6 hrs Adjustable time: 0.5 hr to 24 hrs	60°C

Appendix 2: Recipes Index

Printed in Great Britain
by Amazon